Playing
F
Sha

Twelfth Night
FOR KIDS

(The melodramatic version!)

For 9-20+ actors, or kids of all ages who want to have fun!
Creatively modified by
Brendan P. Kelso and Khara C. Oliver
Cover illustrated by Shana Lopez
Special Contributor: Asif Zamir

3 Melodramatic Modifications of Shakespeare's Play
for 3 different group sizes:

9-10+

11-15+

15-20+

Table Of Contents

Foreward..Pg 3

9-10+ Actors..Pg 7

11-15+ Actors...Pg 26

15-20+ Actors...Pg 47

About the Authors...Pg 69

For my family, with love
- KCO

K-dawg, thanks for keeping the dream alive!
- BPK

Playing with Plays™ – Shakespeare's Twelfth Night– for Kids

Copyright © 2004-2012 by Brendan P. Kelso, Playing with Publishing

All rights reserved. No part of this book may be reproduced in any form or by any electronic or mechanical means, including photocopying, recording, information storage or retrieval systems now known or to be invented, without permission in writing from the publisher. Except by a reviewer, who may quote brief passages in a review, written for inclusion within a periodical. Any members of education institutions wishing to photocopy part or all of the work for classroom use, or publishers, who would like to obtain permission to include the work in an anthology, should send their inquiries to the publisher. We monitor the internet for cases of piracy and copyright infringement/violations. We will pursue all cases within the full extent of the law.

Whenever a Playing With Plays play is produced, the following must be included on all programs, printing and advertising for the play: © Brendan P. Kelso, Playing with Publishing. www.PlayingWithPlays.com. All rights reserved.

CAUTION: Professionals and amateurs are hereby warned that these plays are subject to a royalty. They are fully protected, in whole, in part, or in any form under the copyright laws of the United States, Canada, the British Empire, and all other countries of the Copyright Union, and is subject to royalty. All rights, including professional, amateur, motion picture, radio, television, recitation, public reading, internet, and any method of photographic reproduction are strictly reserved. For performance rights contACT Playing with Plays:

www.PlayingWithPlays.com

Printed in the United States of America

Published by: Playing with Publishing

ISBN: 1466224037
ISBN: 978-1466224032

Foreword

When I was in high school there was something about Shakespeare that appealed to me. Not that I understood it mind you, but there were clear scenes and images that always stood out in my mind. Romeo & Juliet, "Romeo, Romeo; wherefore art thou Romeo?"; Julius Caesar, "Et tu Brute"; Macbeth, "Double, Double, toil and trouble"; Hamlet, "to be or not to be"; A Midsummer Night's Dream, all I remember about this was a wickedly cool fairy and something about a guy turning into a donkey that I thought was pretty funny. It was not until I started analyzing Shakespeare's plays as an actor that I realized one very important thing, I still didn't understand them. Seriously though, it's tough enough for adults, let alone kids. Then it hit me, why don't I make a version that kids could perform, but make it easy for them to understand with a splash of Shakespeare lingo mixed in? And viola! A melodramatic masterpiece was created!

The entire purpose of this book is to instill the love of acting and Shakespeare into kids. I initially wrote my first Shakespeare play (Hamlet) to teach a few kids how to have fun with Shakespeare. It has evolved into a revolving door of new and returning kids constantly wanting more and more Shakespeare, from kids asking for the entire Shakespeare anthology for Christmas to writing a report in their 2nd grade class on heroes and choosing Shakespeare. Shakespeare is difficult enough when you are an adult, let alone a teenager (I didn't have a clue what Julius Caeser was about, except for "Et tu Brute!"). But for kids, most people (those calling themselves "adults" mind you) told me to forget it,

PlayingWithPlays.com

"you can't teach kids Shakespeare". Well, I will have you know, that not only do these kids love Shakespeare now, they want more of it! And when you have children who have a passion for something, they will start to teach themselves, with or without school.

THE PLAYS: There are 3 plays within this book, for three different group sizes. The reason: to allow educators or parents to get the story across to their children regardless of the size of their group. Experienced actor variation: If you read any Shakespeare play as an actor you will notice one very common occurrence – NO STAGE DIRECTIONS. Okay, it happens occasionally, but it's very rare. Any actor with creative skills will tell you that this is a wonderful thing: it leaves full interpretation to the actor. Therefore, for the children who wish to explore their creative side, I suggest taking the play and whiting out ALL of the stage directions, allowing for the more experienced actors to be as creative as they want to be.

These plays are intended for pure fun. Please DO NOT have the kids learn these lines verbatim, that would be a complete waste of creativity. But do have them basically know their lines and improvise wherever they want as long as it pertains to telling the story, because that is the goal of an actor: to tell the story. In A Midsummer Night's Dream, I once had a student playing Quince question me about one of her lines, "but in the actual story, didn't the Mechanicals state that 'they would hang us'?" I thought for a second and realized that she had read the story with her mom, and she was right. So I let her add the line she wanted and it added that much more

4   PlayingWithPlays.com

fun, it made the play theirs. I have had kids throw water on the audience, run around the audience, sit in the audience, lose their pumpkin pants (size 30 around a size 15 doesn't work very well, but makes for some great humor!) and most importantly, die all over the stage. The kids love it.

I have a basic formula that I use for these plays:
Day 1: I perform my own solo 5-minute Shakespeare play (I am totally winded by the end of it, because I have been all over the set and have died a few times if I can fit it in); we all read through the play to-gether (randomly handing out parts); then auditions – and all auditions MUST include the actors best dieing scenes (they love this the most and will line up again and again to die on stage); the other is for the screams, they love this too, but don't forget to bring earplugs, they will be incredibly loud for both girls and boys since not all have come of age yet.
Day 2: Parts are given out; we read through the play again with our new parts; start blocking
Day 3: finish blocking; rehearse
Day 4: rehearse-no scripts
Day 5: rehearse; try on costumes, and dress rehearsal
Day 6: 2 Dress rehearsals and then performance.
This can easily be stretched to an 8 day course with the 2 extra days used for more rehearsal; set design; invitation creation; makeup practice; etc. As any director will tell you, actors can always use more rehearsal.

THE BARD'S WORK: As you read through the plays, there are several lines that are highlighted. These are actual lines from Shakespeare's text. I am a little more particular about the kids saying these lines verbatim. We need to do these correctly because we don't want to upset Willie. I find that there are many benefits to having these lines in there:

1. Kids are so cute when they are spouting Shakespeare.
2. Parents love to know that their kids are learning actual Shakespeare verbiage.
3. Most lines are very famous lines that they will come across later in life (to be or not to be; Romeo, Romeo, wherefore art thou; double, double toil and trouble; etc.)
4. The kids tend to feel they are more important when they are saying Shakespeare's lines.
5. The lines are easy to understand, giving the kids confidence that they will understand more Shakespeare lines later in life.

One last note: if you loved our plays, want to tell the world how much your kids loved performing Shakespeare, or are just a fan of Shakespeare, then hop on our website and have fun:

PlayingWithPlays.com

Oh yeah, and don't forget to sign up on our mailing list (emails rarely happen anyway) and we will give you insider information on new launches, book signings, speaking engagements, and some cool book discounts!

With these notes I bid you adieu, have fun, and good luck!

The 10-Minute or so Twelfth Night
By William Shakespeare
Creatively modified by Brendan P. Kelso and Khara C. Oliver
9-10+ Actors

CAST OF CHARACTERS:

ORSINO: a duke, loves Olivia

VIOLA: girl pretending to be a boy named Cesario

SEBASTIAN: Viola's twin brother (they look alike!)

LADY OLIVIA: loves Cesario (that's Viola. Confused yet?)

SIR TOBY BELCH: uncle to Olivia (likes to belch!)

SIR ANDREW: friend to Toby; likes Olivia

THE CLOWN: funny guy (a fool)

*MALVOLIO: Olivia's servant with funny socks

ANTONIO: Sebastian's friend, enemy of Orsino

*POLICEMAN: a policeman

*The same actor can play Malvolio and Policeman

LORDS and LADIES of the court can be extras as needed

PROLOGUE

(Enter VIOLA and SEBASTIAN, wearing identical clothes so the audience knows they are twins)

SEBASTIAN: *(To audience with VIOLA standing next to him)* She is my twin sister.

VIOLA: He is my twin brother.

SEBASTIAN: Enjoy the show! *(All exit)*

ACT 1 SCENE 1

(Enter ORSINO)

ORSINO: If music be the food of love, play on! *(Talks to a picture of Olivia he is holding)* Oh, Olivia...why won't you notice me? Why? I mean, I'm sorry that your brother died and you decided to hide and cry for the next SEVEN years, but why be sad when I love you so, so, SO much! *(ORSINO looks depressed, Sighs loudly and exits)*

ACT 1 SCENE 2

(Enter VIOLA)

VIOLA: *(To audience)* Whew! I just survived a terrible shipwreck! But, O my poor twin brother, Sebastian, he may have drowned. That stinks! Oh well! *(Looks around)* I'm in the city of Illyria, ruled by the handsome, noble Duke Orsino. I hear he's single and cute, yes! And in love with Olivia, bummer. Hey! I have a great idea! I'll disguise myself as a man, and I'll serve this duke. He'll like me 'cause I'm a really good singer. *(Singing in a really low voice)* Row, row, row your boat...

(Viola exits while singing)

ACT 1 SCENE 3

(Enter SIR TOBY BELCH, and SIR ANDREW)

TOBY: Sir Andrew, what is with my niece Olivia? I know her brother just died, but she is taking this "mourning" thing waaaaay too seriously. I mean, seven years of being sad, really? Being so sad all the time is not good for your health. *(Belches)*

ANDREW: *(To audience)* They don't call him Sir Toby BELCH for nothing! *(To Toby)* Since Olivia is being such a bummer, I'll ride home tomorrow, Sir Toby.

TOBY: Pourquoi, my dear knight?

ANDREW: What is "pourquoi"?

TOBY: Poor-kwah means "why" in French. Makes me sound smart, doesn't it?

ANDREW: Oh, I wish I had paid more attention in school!

TOBY: Andrew, please stay. Olivia could snap out of it, and who knows, she might actually think you're cute. *(Shakes head at audience)*

ANDREW: Oh, alright, I'll stay a month longer. But let's go dancing! I'm a really good dancer. *(He starts to dance like a crazy man)*

TOBY: *(Pumps his fist in the air to the beat)* Sir Andrew in the HOUSE! Go Andy! Go Andy! Go! Go! Go Andy!

(All exit dancing)

ACT 1 SCENE 4

(Enter ORSINO and VIOLA, who is dressed as a man "Cesario")

ORSINO: Cesario!

VIOLA: *(Looks around for Cesario before remembering SHE is Cesario now)* Uh, yes, my lord?

ORSINO: Go tell Olivia how much I like her, no... LOVE her.... Be not denied access, stand at her doors, and stay there till she talks to you.

VIOLA: Orsino, what happened to seven years? 1, 2, 3....

ORSINO: Ugh! Seven, schmevin! *(Stamps foot).* I don't care. Be clamorous. Be loud. Be rude. Just don't take no for an answer!

VIOLA: When I see her, what then?

ORSINO: Tell her I love her. Act like me and say smart things.

VIOLA: And you can't go because....

ORSINO: 'Cause I'm a duke! I don't do anything for myself. And you're soooo *(Confused suddenly)* pretty? Er...handsome. *(Starts looking funny at VIOLA)* Just go!

VIOLA: Fine, fine. I'll do my best to woo your lady. *(To audience pointing at ORSINO)* But it's going to be so hard! Because after these last three days of tying his shoes, I TOTALLY want to marry him myself! *(All exit)*

ACT 1 SCENE 5

(Enter SIR TOBY and CLOWN)

CLOWN: Those that are fools, let them use their talents.

TOBY: What?

CLOWN: You know, "fool" another name for a clown.... *(With two thumbs pointed at himself)*

(Enter OLIVIA)

OLIVIA: *(Using air quotes)* Go away, Clown, take the "fool" away.

CLOWN: But Olivia, I can make you laugh! *(Makes a silly face)* And you need to laugh because you're acting so sad... give me another chance, pretty please? *(Falls on ground and pretends to cry)* See, I'm funny!

OLIVIA: Yes, but you are funnier off stage, now go.

CLOWN: BORING....

(Exit CLOWN and TOBY; enter MALVOLIO)

MALVOLIO: Lady Olivia, there is at the gate a young gentleman who much desires to speak with you.

OLIVIA: Nope.

MALVOLIO: Seriously, I told him you were sick. I told him you were asleep. I told him you were sick in your sleep. The dude is NOT leaving.

OLIVIA: Fine. Let him approach.

(Throws a blanket over her head)

(MALVOLIO exits; Enter VIOLA disguised as Cesario)

VIOLA: Um, hi. Are you Olivia?

OLIVIA: Maybe.

VIOLA: Well I heard Olivia is the most radiant, exquisite, and unmatchable beauty, like, EVER.

OLIVIA: That would be me.

VIOLA: *(To audience)* Now we're getting somewhere. *(To OLIVIA)* AHEM: Orsino loves you with all of his heart.

OLIVIA: Are you a comedian? *(Takes off blanket)*

VIOLA: Wow, you are pretty.

OLIVIA: I know.

VIOLA: I see you what you are, you are too proud.

OLIVIA: Look, I know Orsino is young, noble, and rich, but I cannot love him.

VIOLA: *(To audience)* Well, I don't get it, but hey, I tried. Farewell, fair cruelty! *(VIOLA exits)*

OLIVIA: *(To audience)* OMG! Isn't he perfect!? Oh, I am so in L-O-V-E with that boy! *(Yells off stage)* Malvolio!

(Enter MALVOLIO)

OLIVIA: Run after him and tell him he has to come back tomorrow!

(MALVOLIO exits, OLIVIA skips off stage giggling)

ACT 2 SCENE 1

(Enter ANTONIO and SEBASTIAN)

SEBASTIAN: Thanks for saving my life Antonio. Gotta go, see ya later!

ANTONIO: Whoa, Sebastian. Can I go with you? You're my new best friend!

SEBASTIAN: Nah. I am a really bummed that my twin sister, Viola, drowned some hour before you found me.

ANTONIO: That's awful. You really shouldn't be alone. Let me be your servant.

SEBASTIAN: Sure, that sounds cool, come on! *(All exit)*

ACT 2 SCENE 2

(Enter VIOLA with MALVOLIO following behind)

MALVOLIO: Excuse me, sir! Wait up!

VIOLA: Yes?

MALVOLIO: Olivia says you HAVE to come back tomorrow.

VIOLA: I really don't want to.

MALVOLIO: Well, I don't think you really have a choice. See ya! *(MALVOLIO exits)*

VIOLA: *(To audience)* Uh-oh. I think Olivia has a crush on me. This is getting confusing. So, let's review: I'm in love with Orsino *(ORSINO pops his head out from offstage and waves at audience)*, he's in love with Olivia *(OLIVIA pops her head out from offstage and waves at audience)*, and she's in love with me! O time, thou must untangle this, not I, it is too hard a knot for me to untie! *(In a whisper voice)* that means only time will fix this! *(Exits)*

12   PlayingWithPlays.com

ACT 2 SCENE 3

(Enter TOBY and ANDREW having a belching contest, and CLOWN follows)

CLOWN: STOP THAT!!! It's disgusting!

TOBY: *(Belches and smiles at CLOWN)* What a great party! Let's stay up the rest of the night and celebrate!

ANDREW: Our lives consist of eating and drinking! To be up late is to be up late! *(Belches to Clown)*

CLOWN: You guys are SOOOO gross!

(Enter MALVOLIO)

TOBY & ANDREW: *(To audience)* Uh-oh, Malvolio!

MALVOLIO: I should have known it was you fools making all this racket. Have you no wit, manners, nor honesty, but to gabble like tinkers at this time of night?

ANDREW: Oh, puh-lease...What does "gabble" mean anyway?

MALVOLIO: To talk...

CLOWN: And belch!

MALVOLIO: ...and talk...on, and on, and on... Look, Toby, Olivia told me that if you don't start acting like a proper gentleman, she is very willing to bid you farewell, even if you are her uncle.

TOBY: Oh, I'm soooo scared! Listen, you goody-two-shoes, leave us alone.

MALVOLIO: You people are hopeless.

(MALVOLIO exits)

ANDREW: What a fuddy-duddy.

TOBY: Listen, I have an evil plan! Let's play a joke on Malvolio!

PlayingWithPlays.com

13

ANDREW: What wilt thou do?

TOBY: I will have one of the servants write a romantic letter from "Olivia" about how she's in love with Malvolio. He'll believe it and when he finds out the truth, he'll feel like a total blockhead.

ANDREW: Brilliant! You are a genius, Sir Toby!

(All exit; TOBY and ANDREW start belching as they exit)

ACT 2 SCENE 4

(Enter ORSINO and VIOLA)

ORSINO: Let me tell you something, Cesario, if ever thou shalt love, you will finally know what it's like to be me right now. All I can think of is Olivia. Olivia, Olivia, Olivia! *(Sighs and looks at VIOLA and pauses for effect)* My gut tells me you've fallen in love with someone, am I right?

VIOLA: *(Surprised)* Well, kind of. *(To audience, VIOLA starts pointing at ORSINO)*

ORSINO: That's great! What kind of girl is she?

VIOLA: *(Glancing at the audience)* She's, um, like you.

ORSINO: She is not worth thee, then. How old is she?

VIOLA: *(Still looking at the audience)* About your years, my lord. *(To the audience)* and size, height, weight...smell....

ORSINO: Too old, by heaven! Enough about you, let's talk about me. Where were we, oh yes! Olivia!!! Go and tell her I care only for her.

VIOLA: Sorry, Orsino, but she really doesn't love you. I don't even think she LIKES you.

ORSINO: I will make her love me. I know I can.

VIOLA: *(Sighs)* If you say so. Sir, shall I to this lady, Olivia?

ORSINO: Yes! And give her this jewel.

VIOLA: Right! Off I go! *(All exit)*

ACT 2 SCENE 5

(Enter TOBY and ANDREW)

TOBY: Come on Sir Andrew, let's watch Malvolio's reaction to "the love letter." *(Throws a letter on the ground)*

ANDREW: I wouldn't miss this for the world!

(They hide; enter Malvolio)

MALVOLIO: I am feeling very lucky today. What's this? *(Picks up letter and opens it)* Why, it's a letter from Olivia! I wonder who it's for? *(Reads)* "Jove knows I love, but who?" Sounds very Shakespearean.

ANDREW: Can you believe this guy?

TOBY: Shhhh! This is good stuff!

MALVOLIO: *(Reads)* " Malvolio, I don't care if you're my servant. Some are born great, some achieve greatness, and some have greatness thrust upon 'em. Please wear those ridiculous yellow stockings that I love. I love you!" Woo-hoo! Oh, I am so happy! She loves me! Oh, to be Count Malvolio!

(MALVOLIO exits dancing and singing; TOBY and ANDREW laugh)

TOBY: That was amazing. He believed every word! Let's go watch him make a fool of himself around Olivia. He'll come to her in those ugly yellow stockings that she hates, and she'll be totally annoyed by his happiness.

ANDREW: Let's go! *(They high five each other and exit)*

PlayingWithPlays.com

ACT 3 SCENE 1

(Enter VIOLA, TOBY and ANDREW)

TOBY: *(To VIOLA)* Hello there! My niece, Olivia, would like to talk to you.

VIOLA: Well, that's why I'm here; I want to talk to her, too.

TOBY: Great! Taste your legs, sir. Put them to motion.

VIOLA: Taste your legs?

TOBY: Yeah. You know, hurry up. Don't you speak Shakespeare?

(Enter OLIVIA)

VIOLA: Hi Olivia. Can I speak to you... *(Looks around at everybody)* in private?

OLIVIA: Of course. *(Clears her throat loudly; TOBY, ANDREW exit)*

OLIVIA: What is your name, anyway?

VIOLA: Cesario. But I'm here to talk about...

OLIVIA: I know, I know. Orsino! Yuck. I beg you never speak again of him. Let's talk about me instead. *(Pause)* I love you. *(Uncomfortable silence)*

VIOLA: I pity you.

OLIVIA: *(To the audience)* I guess that's better than nothing. This is a bit embarrassing... OK, you can leave now!!!

VIOLA: Great! Bye!

OLIVIA: *(Grabs VIOLA)* No wait! Stay!

VIOLA: *(To audience)* Go! Stay! What is wrong with this lady?

OLIVIA: Could you just TRY to love me? A little bit? Please?

VIOLA: I swear to you that I will never love you! EVER. See ya later. *(VIOLA exits)*

OLIVIA: Bummer! *(Exits)*

ACT 3 SCENE 2

(Enter TOBY and ANDREW)

ANDREW: *(To TOBY)* Olivia is never going to notice me. I'm leaving town.

TOBY: *(Belches)* Wait! Maybe she's just trying to make you jealous. Did you think of that? She wants you to win her over. You know what would really impress her? A duel! You should totally challenge Cesario!

ANDREW: I don't know...

TOBY: There is no way but this, Sir Andrew. You've got to fight for her.

ANDREW: I'll do it! I'm going to go challenge Cesario right now! *(They exit)*

ACT 3 SCENE 3

(Enter SEBASTIAN and ANTONIO)

SEBASTIAN: Thanks for coming with me, Antonio. You're a great friend.

ANTONIO: No problem. Listen, want to find a hotel? In the south suburbs, we can stay at the Elephant hotel.

SEBASTIAN: The Elephant? But I didn't bring my trunk! Get it? Elephant? Trunk?

ANTONIO: *(Not laughing)* That was really bad.

SEBASTIAN: It wasn't THAT bad. Anyway...let's go see the sights first! I've never been to Ilyria.

ANTONIO: Sorry, my friend. During the war I stole a lot of their money. So if the wrong people see me here, I could be in a lot of trouble.

SEBASTIAN: Do not then walk too open.

ANTONIO: I'll be careful. But here's some money, go have fun.

SEBASTIAN: Okay. Thanks, Antonio. See you later at the Elephant. *(SEBASTIAN holds arm out in front of face like a trunk and trumpets like an elephant; ANTONIO looks at the audience and shakes head. They exit)*

ACT 3 SCENE 4

(Enter OLIVIA and TOBY)

OLIVIA: Where's Malvolio? He is sad and civil, just what I need right now to take my mind off of Cesario.

TOBY: He's coming, but in very strange manner. He is sure possessed.

OLIVIA: What's wrong with him?

TOBY: I think he's gone crazy. Here he comes!

(Enter MALVOLIO)

MALVOLIO: *(To OLIVIA)* Sweet lady, ho ho!

OLIVIA: Why are you smiling? I want you to be sad.

MALVOLIO: *(Smiling)* I'm following your letter, see? *(Points to his yellow socks)* I'm seizing the day, Olivia! Carpe diem!

OLIVIA: You're right, Sir Toby, the young gentleman has obviously gone insane. Sir Toby, watch over Malvolio until he feels better. I hope he's not crazy forever. *(OLIVIA exits)*

MALVOLIO: *(To audience)* She must love me! She's having her uncle take care of me! This is SO great.

(Enter ANDREW)

ANDREW: How is't with you, Malvolio?

MALVOLIO: Leave me alone.

18 PlayingWithPlays.com

TOBY: We need to be careful with him. He might be dangerous!

(They start backing away from MALVOLIO)

MALVOLIO: I don't have time for this. I'm leaving.

(MALVOLIO exits)

ANDREW: Why, we shall make him mad indeed.

TOBY: The house will be the quieter.

ANDREW: Not to change the subject, but here's the challenge, read it.

TOBY: *(Reads letter)* "Cesario, I don't know you, but I really don't like you and I think we should duel. Sincerely, Sir Andrew." *(Sarcastically)* Well, that should terrify him. I'll deliver your letter. Go wait for him in the garden. As soon as you see him, attack him with your sword!

ANDREW: Got it! *(ANDREW exits)*

TOBY: I can't deliver this letter; it's...dumb. I will deliver his challenge by word of mouth.

(Enter VIOLA)

TOBY: Cesario! There's a pretty angry knight waiting for you outside. Thy assailant is quick, skillful and deadly, and wants to kill you.

VIOLA: What?! Somebody's mad at me? I didn't do anything!

TOBY: Come on, just go out and fight him! Just to warn you, this knight is the most skillful, bloody and fatal opposite that you could have possibly found in any part of Illyria. *(Winks at audience)* Wait here.

VIOLA: *(To audience)* I hate fighting.

(ANDREW enters, TOBY runs over to him)

TOBY: You better prepare yourself. They say he is the best in this kingdom!

ANDREW: Uh-oh. I'll not meddle with him.

TOBY: I don't think you can get out of it now.

(TOBY pushes ANDREW towards VIOLA)

TOBY: LET'S DO THIS!!

(VIOLA and ANDREW pull out their swords and start walking towards each other with their eyes closed; Enter ANTONIO)

ANTONIO: Stop! Put up your sword.

TOBY: Who in the heck are you?

ANTONIO: I'm his friend *(Points to VIOLA).* I'd do anything for him!

TOBY and VIOLA: Huh?

TOBY: Well then, let's fight! *(He pulls out a sword)*

(Enter POLICEMAN)

POLICEMAN: *(Grabs ANTONIO)* This is the man! You are under arrest for stealing our money! Let's go!

ANTONIO: *(To VIOLA)* See, I told you they don't like me. Listen, do you still have that money I gave you?

VIOLA: What money, sir? I have no idea who you are!

ANTONIO: Seriously? You're going to pretend not to know me? This is ridiculous! *(To the POLICEMAN)* You see, I rescued him when he was drowning and have really been a good friend to him.

POLICEMAN: Waa, waa, waa.

ANTONIO: *(To VIOLA)* Thanks a lot, Sebastian.

(POLICEMAN takes ANTONIO away)

VIOLA: *(To audience)* Wow. He was really upset. He nam'd Sebastian, my brother's name? Is he alive?! How cool would that be!

(VIOLA exits)

TOBY: I can't believe Cesario just let his friend be taken away like that!

ANDREW: I know! Now I really want to go beat him up!

TOBY: Well, what are we waiting for? Let's go get him!

(All exit)

ACT 4 SCENE 1

(Enter SEBASTIAN, ANDREW and TOBY)

ANDREW: *(To SEBASTIAN)* Ah-HA! I knew I'd find you, Cesario! *(ANDREW draws his sword and pokes SEBASTIAN)* There's for you.

SEBASTIAN: *(Pulls his sword and begins fighting with ANDREW)* Why there's for thee, and there, and there! Holy cow! Is everyone in Ilyria crazy? I swear I don't know any of you people!

(TOBY sneaks up and grabs SEBASTIAN from behind)

TOBY: Gotcha!

SEBASTIAN: Let me go! This is SO not cool!

TOBY: *(Belches in SEBASTIAN'S ear)* No way, José.

(SEBASTIAN breaks free and TOBY draws his sword; Enter OLIVIA)

OLIVIA: Stop this right now! Uncle Toby, leave poor Cesario alone and get out of my sight!

TOBY: Sorry, Olivia.

(TOBY and ANDREW exit)

OLIVIA: Those boys are so childish with all their fighting. Why don't you come back to my house for a while?

SEBASTIAN: *(To audience)* She called me "Cesario" too, but she's really cute, so I think I'll go with her. *(To OLIVIA)* Madam, I will. *(They exit)*

ACT 4 SCENE 2

(Enter CLOWN and MALVOLIO. MALVOLIO'S hands are tied and he is blindfolded)

CLOWN: What's up, crazy guy?

MALVOLIO: Is that you, Clown? Can you help me?

CLOWN: Sorry, I don't help crazy people.

MALVOLIO: I'm not crazy, you fool! Sir Toby tied me up! *(Starts crying like a baby)* I want my mommy!

CLOWN: *(to Audience)* Well, this is embarrassing. *(To MALVOLIO)* Okay, okay, I'll help you. But tell me true, are you not mad indeed?

MALVOLIO: *(Still crying)* Believe me, I am not. I tell thee true. Waaaaaaa!

CLOWN: *(Unties MALVOLIO and removes blindfold)* ALRIGHT! Look, Sir Toby and Sir Andrew played a joke on you. Olivia never wrote that letter.

MALVOLIO: WHAT?! I'll be revenged on the whole pack of them! They have done me wrong!

(MALVOLIO storms off stage in a rage; CLOWN shrugs his shoulders)

CLOWN: *(To audience)* I must admit, it was kind of funny!

ACT 4 SCENE 3

(Enter SEBASTIAN)

SEBASTIAN: This is the air, that is the glorious sun. This MUST be a dream! WOW, Olivia loves me! I don't even care that she keeps calling me Cesario and I met her this morning!

(Enter OLIVIA)

OLIVIA: I don't mean to rush you, Cesario, but I found a priest who agreed to marry us....now. What do you say?

SEBASTIAN: Now? Sure, why not? Let's get married! Lead the way to the good father!

(They exit very excited and high fiving)

ACT 5 SCENE 1

(Enter ORSINO and VIOLA)

ORSINO: Today's the day, Cesario! Olivia will finally realize that I'm the man for her.

VIOLA: Hey look! There's the guy who got dragged away by the police!

(Enter ANTONIO and POLICEMAN)

ORSINO: That face of his I do remember well. Hey, you stole our money!

POLICEMAN: Yeah, he's a stinky pirate.

ANTONIO: I am not a pirate, and I am not stinky! I'm only here because I rescued HIM from drowning *(Points to VIOLA)*, and now he's pretending that he doesn't know who I am! *(Whines)* And he was my best friend.

ORSINO: When came he to this town?

ANTONIO: Got here this morning.

ORSINO: This morning! Then you really have lost your mind. Cesario's been serving me for three months!

(Enter OLIVIA)

OLIVIA: Orsino...you're here again?! I. Don't. Like. You. Okay?

ORSINO: Still so cruel?

OLIVIA: Still so constant, lord.

ORSINO: Fine then, I'm leaving. Come on, Cesario.

OLIVIA: Where do you think you're going, Cesario?!

VIOLA: With Orsino. I love him.

ORSINO: Let's go, Cesario!

OLIVIA: Cesario, husband, stay!

VIOLA: *(Whispers)* Husband?

ORSINO: Husband?!

OLIVIA: Yes, HUSBAND! Cesario and I were married earlier today.

(Enter ANDREW, TOBY and CLOWN, all moaning and covered in bandages)

ANDREW: AH! My head! *(Grabs head)*

TOBY: AH! My leg!! *(Grabs leg and belches)*

CLOWN: *(Sarcastically)* AH! My brain!

OLIVIA: Who did this to you?

ANDREW: Cesario! We took him for a coward, but he's the very devil incardinate. *(Points to VIOLA)* There he is!

VIOLA: What are you talking about? I never hurt you.

TOBY: Are you kidding me? You just bashed him in the head!

OLIVIA: Enough! Fool, get him to bed, and let his hurt be looked to. All of you! Go!

(CLOWN pushes TOBY & ANDREW offstage; enter SEBAS-TIAN)

SEBASTIAN: *(To OLIVIA)* Sorry I'm late, dear wife, but I got into a fight with your uncle. *(Notices ANTONIO)* Antonio! Hey buddy! Where on earth have you been?

(Everyone looks at SEBASTIAN, then at VIOLA, then at SEBASTIAN again)

ORSINO: One face, one voice, one habit, and two persons!

ANTONIO: Um...if you're Sebastian, then who is THAT? *(Points at VIOLA)*

SEBASTIAN: Do I stand there? I never had a brother. I had a sister, but she drowned.

VIOLA: No she didn't! *(Takes off her disguise)* It's me!

SEBASTIAN: Viola! Sister!

(They run to each other and perform a long, elaborate secret handshake).

OLIVIA and ORSINO: You're a GIRL?

VIOLA: One hundred percent!

SEBASTIAN: *(To OLIVIA)* See! It all worked out. You fell in love with my sister, but in the end you got me! *(Laughs)*

(Everyone except VIOLA starts laughing)

ORSINO: *(To VIOLA)* It's okay, Cesario, er, I mean...Viola, I think you're super cute! So cute, that I want to marry you!

VIOLA: Yes! Score!

ORSINO: Indeed!

CLOWN: Let the celebrating begin! *(Begins to sing a popular love song; Everyone on stage begins to dance to CLOWN'S song, dancing their way off the stage)*

THE END

The 15-Minute or so Twelfth Night

By William Shakespeare
Creatively modified by Brendan P. Kelso and Khara C. Oliver

11-15+ Actors

CAST OF CHARACTERS:

ORSINO: a duke, loves Olivia

VIOLA: girl pretending to be a boy named Cesario

SEBASTIAN: Viola's twin brother (they look alike!)

LADY OLIVIA: loves Cesario (that's Viola. Confused yet?)

SIR TOBY BELCH: uncle to Olivia (likes to belch!)

***SIR ANDREW:** friend to Toby; likes Olivia

MARIA: lady in waiting (for what, we are not sure)

THE CLOWN: funny guy (a fool)

*MALVOLIO:** Olivia's servant with funny socks

FABIAN: Olivia's other servant

ANTONIO: Sebastian's friend, enemy of Orsino

VALENTINE: Orsino's servant

***SEA CAPTAIN:** a sea captain

*POLICEMAN:** a policeman

***MUSICIAN:** person who plays music

*The same actor can play Malvolio and Policeman
**The same actor can play Valentine and Fabian
***The same actor can play Sea Captain, Sir Andrew, and another Musician

MUSICIANS, LORDS and LADIES of the court can be extras as needed

PROLOGUE

(Enter VIOLA and SEBASTIAN, wearing identical clothes so the audience knows they are twins)

SEBASTIAN: *(To audience with VIOLA standing next to him)* She is my twin sister.

VIOLA: He is my twin brother.

SEBASTIAN: Enjoy the show! *(All exit)*

ACT 1 SCENE 1

(Enter ORSINO and MUSICIAN)

ORSINO: If music be the food of love, play on! *(ORSINO looks depressed)*

MUSICIAN: La, la la la la…. *(While dancing a bit crazy, then exit)*

ORSINO: *(Starts talking to a picture of Olivia)* Oh, Olivia… why won't you notice me? Why?

(Enter VALENTINE)

ORSINO: How now, what news from her?

VALENTINE: Sorry, man. Olivia's brother just died, and she is so bummed, that she decided to hide and cry for the next seven years.

ORSINO: Seven years? Are you sure you don't mean seven days, or maybe even seven months?

VALENTINE: Nope, SEVEN YEARS!

ORSINO: Seriously? Wow! *(To audience)* You have to admire that kind of dedication. I think I love her even more now. *(Sighs again, all exit)*

ACT 1 SCENE 2

(Enter VIOLA and SEA CAPTAIN)

VIOLA: Whew! We just survived a terrible shipwreck! O my poor twin brother, Sebastian, may have drowned. *(To Sea Captain)* Captain, do you think there's any chance he made it?

SEA CAPTAIN: Could be, Viola, let's stay optimistic.

VIOLA: Where are we?

SEA CAPTAIN: This is Illyria, lady, ruled by the noble Duke Orsino.

VIOLA: Hmmm...I remember hearing that he was single and cute!

SEA CAPTAIN: Yes, but he is in love with the fair Olivia.

VIOLA: *(To audience)* Hey! I'm going to disguise myself like a man, and I'll serve this duke. He'll like me 'cause I'm a really good singer. *(Singing in a really low voice)* Row, row, row your boat...

SEA CAPTAIN: Sure! *(Covering his ears because it sounds so bad)* But, ahhh, do me a favor, don't sing... just do the disguise thing. TRUST ME! *(All exit)*

ACT 1 SCENE 3

(Enter SIR TOBY BELCH, MARIA and SIR ANDREW)

TOBY: *(Belches)* Maria, what is with my niece Olivia? She is taking this "mourning" thing waaaaay too seriously. Being so sad all the time is not good for your health.

MARIA: Gross, quit belching Sir Toby BELCH.

ANDREW: He can't help it if that's his name! Sir Toby Belch!

TOBY: That's right, sweet Sir Andrew!

MARIA: Whatever. Look you two, why don't you just get on with your night of silliness? I have better things to do.

(MARIA exits)

ANDREW: Since your niece, Olivia, is being such a bummer, I'll ride home tomorrow, Sir Toby.

TOBY: Pourquoi, my dear knight?

ANDREW: What is "pourquoi"?

TOBY: Poor-kwah means "why" in French. Makes me sound smart, doesn't it?

ANDREW: Oh, I wish I had paid more attention in school!

TOBY: Andrew, please stay. Olivia could snap out of it, and who knows, she might actually think you're cute. *(Shakes head at audience)*

ANDREW: Oh, alright, I'll stay a month longer. But let's go dancing! I'm a really good dancer. *(He starts to dance like a crazy man)*

TOBY: *(Pumps his fist in the air)* Sir Andrew in the HOUSE! Go Andy! Go Andy! Go! Go! Go Andy! *(All exit dancing)*

ACT 1 SCENE 4

(Enter VALENTINE and VIOLA dressed as a man "Cesario")

VALENTINE: Cesario!

VIOLA: *(In a fake man-voice and winks at audience)* Yes?

VALENTINE: Listen, the duke Orsino thinks you're cool.

VIOLA: Really? I thank you. Here comes the count now.

(Enter ORSINO)

ORSINO: Cesario! Go tell Olivia how much I like her, no... LOVE her....Be not denied access, stand at her doors, and stay there till she talks to you.

VIOLA: Orsino, what happened to seven years? 1, 2, 3....

ORSINO: Ugh! Seven, schmevin! *(Stamps foot)*. I don't care. Be clamorous. Be loud. Be rude. Just don't take no for an answer!

VIOLA: When I see her, what then?

ORSINO: Tell her I love her. Act like me and say smart things.

VIOLA: And you can't go because....

ORSINO: 'Cause I'm a duke! I don't do anything for myself. *(Snaps his fingers at VALENTINE and points to his untied shoe. VALENTINE hurries to tie it)* And you're soooo *(Confused suddenly)* pretty? Er...handsome. *(Starts looking funny at VIOLA)* Just go!

VIOLA: Fine, fine. I'll do my best to woo your lady. *(To audience pointing at ORSINO)* But it's going to be so hard! Because after these last three days of tying his shoes, I TOTALLY want to marry him myself! *(All exit)*

ACT 1 SCENE 5

(Enter MARIA and CLOWN)

CLOWN: Those that are fools, let them use their talents.

MARIA: What?

CLOWN: You know, "fool" another name for a clown.... *(With two thumbs pointed at himself)*

MARIA: You are so silly; here comes my lady, Olivia.

(Enter OLIVIA)

OLIVIA: *(using air quotes)* Go away, Clown, take the "fool" away.

CLOWN: But I can make you laugh! *(Makes a silly face)* And you need to laugh because you're acting so sad...give me another chance, pretty please? *(Falls on ground and pretends to cry)* See, I'm funny!

OLIVIA: Yes, but you are funnier off stage, now go.

CLOWN: BORING....

(Exit CLOWN and MARIA; enter MALVOLIO)

MALVOLIO: Lady Olivia, there is at the gate a young gentleman who much desires to speak with you.

OLIVIA: Nope.

MALVOLIO: Seriously, I told him you were sick. I told him you were asleep. I told him you were sick in your sleep. The dude is NOT leaving.

OLIVIA: Fine. Let him approach.

(Throws a blanket over her head)

(MALVOLIO exits; Enter VIOLA disguised as Cesario)

VIOLA: Um, hi. Are you Olivia?

OLIVIA: Maybe.

VIOLA: Well I heard Olivia is the most radiant, exquisite, and unmatchable beauty, like, EVER.

OLIVIA: That would be me.

VIOLA: *(To audience)* Now we're getting somewhere. *(To OLIVIA)* AHEM: Orsino loves you with all of his heart.

OLIVIA: Are you a comedian? *(Takes off blanket)*

VIOLA: Wow, you are pretty.

OLIVIA: I know.

VIOLA: I see you what you are, you are too proud.

OLIVIA: Look, I know Orsino is young, noble, and rich, but I cannot love him.

VIOLA: *(To audience)* Well, I don't get it, but hey, I tried. Farewell, fair cruelty! *(VIOLA exits)*

PlayingWithPlays.com   31

OLIVIA: *(To audience)* OMG! Isn't he perfect!? Oh, I am so in L-O-V-E with that boy! *(Yells off stage)* Malvolio!

(Enter MALVOLIO)

OLIVIA: Run after him and tell him he has to come back tomorrow!

(MALVOLIO exits, OLIVIA skips off stage giggling)

ACT 2 SCENE 1

(Enter ANTONIO and SEBASTIAN)

SEBASTIAN: Thanks for saving my life Antonio. Gotta go, see ya later!

ANTONIO: Whoa, Sebastian. Can I go with you? You're my new best friend!

SEBASTIAN: Nah. I am a really bummed that my twin sister, Viola, drowned some hour before you found me.

ANTONIO: That's awful. You really shouldn't be alone. Let me be your servant.

SEBASTIAN: Sure, that sounds cool, come on! *(All exit)*

ACT 2 SCENE 2

(Enter VIOLA with MALVOLIO following behind)

MALVOLIO: Excuse me, sir! Wait up!

VIOLA: Yes?

MALVOLIO: Olivia says you HAVE to come back tomorrow.

VIOLA: I really don't want to.

MALVOLIO: Well, I don't think you really have a choice. See ya! *(MALVOLIO exits)*

VIOLA: *(To audience)* Uh-oh. I think Olivia has a crush on me. This is getting confusing. So, let's review: I'm in love with Orsino *(ORSINO pops his head out from offstage and waves at audience)*, he's in love with Olivia *(OLIVIA pops her* head out from offstage and waves at audience), and she's in love with me! O time, thou must untangle this, not I, it is too hard a knot for me to untie! *(In a whisper voice)* that means only time will fix this! *(Exits)*

ACT 2 SCENE 3

(Enter SIR TOBY BELCH and SIR ANDREW having a belching contest, and CLOWN follows)

CLOWN: STOP THAT!!! It's disgusting!

TOBY: *(Belches and smiles at CLOWN)* What a great party! Let's stay up the rest of the night and celebrate!

ANDREW: Our lives consist of eating and drinking! To be up late is to be up late! *(Belches to Clown)*

CLOWN: You guys are SOOOO gross!

(Enter MARIA)

MARIA: It's three in the morning! If you guys don't keep it quiet, Olivia will send Malvolio to yell at you.

TOBY: *(Sarcastically)* Oh no! Not Malvolio! *(Belches, and shoots a quick glance at CLOWN)*

(Enter MALVOLIO)

TOBY & ANDREW: *(To audience)* Uh-oh, Malvolio!

MALVOLIO: I should have known it was you fools making all this racket. Have you no wit, manners, nor honesty, but to gabble like tinkers at this time of night?

ANDREW: Oh, puh-lease...What does "gabble" mean anyway?

MALVOLIO: To talk...

CLOWN: And belch!

MALVOLIO: ...and talk...on, and on, and on... Look, Toby, Olivia told me that if you don't start acting like a proper gentleman, she is very willing to bid you farewell; even if you are her uncle.

TOBY: Oh, I'm soooo scared! Listen, you goody-two-shoes, leave us alone.

MALVOLIO: You people are hopeless.

(MALVOLIO exits)

ANDREW: What a fuddy-duddy.

MARIA: Listen guys, I have an evil plan! Let's play a joke on Malvolio!

TOBY: What wilt thou do?

MARIA: I will write a romantic letter from Olivia about how she's in love with Malvolio. He'll believe it and when he finds out the truth, he'll feel like a total blockhead.

ANDREW: Brilliant! You are a genius, Maria!

(All exit; TOBY and ANDREW start belching again)

ACT 2 SCENE 4

(Enter ORSINO and VIOLA)

ORSINO: Let me tell you something, Cesario, if ever thou shalt love, you will finally know what it's like to be me right now. All I can think of is Olivia. Olivia, Olivia, Olivia! *(Sighs and looks at VIOLA and pauses for effect)* My gut tells me you've fallen in love with someone, am I right?

VIOLA: *(Surprised)* Well, kind of. *(To audience, VIOLA starts pointing at ORSINO)*

ORSINO: That's great! What kind of girl is she?

VIOLA: *(Glancing at the audience)* She's, um, like you.

ORSINO: She is not worth thee, then. How old is she?

VIOLA: *(Still looking at the audience)* About your years, my lord. *(To the audience)* and size, height, weight...smell....

ORSINO: Too old, by heaven! Enough about you, let's talk about me. Where were we, oh yes! Olivia!!! Go and tell her I care only for her.

VIOLA: Sorry, Orsino, but she really doesn't love you. I don't even think she LIKES you.

ORSINO: I will make her love me. I know I can.

VIOLA: *(Sighs)* If you say so. Sir, shall I to this lady, Olivia?

ORSINO: Yes! And give her this jewel.

VIOLA: Right! Off I go! *(All exit)*

ACT 2 SCENE 5

(Enter TOBY, ANDREW and FABIAN)

TOBY: Come on Fabian, let's watch Malvolio's reaction to "the love letter."

FABIAN: I wouldn't miss this for the world!

(Enter MARIA)

MARIA: Hide! Here comes Malvolio! *(She tosses a letter on the ground; MARIA exits, the men "hide" upstage; Enter MALVOLIO)*

MALVOLIO: I am feeling very lucky today. What's this? *(Picks up letter and opens it)* Why, it's a letter from Olivia! I wonder who it's for? *(Reads)* "Jove knows I love, but who?" Sounds very Shakespearean.

ANDREW: Can you believe this guy?

FABIAN: Shhhh! This is good stuff!

MALVOLIO: *(Reads)* "Malvolio, I don't care if you're my servant. Some are born great, some achieve greatness, and some have greatness thrust upon 'em. Please wear those ridiculous yellow stockings that I love. I love you!" Woo-hoo! Oh, I am so happy! She loves me! Oh, to be Count Malvolio!

PlayingWithPlays.com

35

(MALVOLIO exits dancing and singing; TOBY, ANDREW and FABIAN laugh)

TOBY: Seriously, I could marry Maria for her brilliance.

ANDREW: So could I too!

FABIAN: So could I three!

(Enter MARIA)

MARIA: Does it work upon him?

TOBY: Does it work upon him? If you mean, how did it go, it was amazing. He believed every word!

MARIA: Cool! He'll come to her in those ugly yellow stockings that she hates, and she'll be totally annoyed by his happiness.

ANDREW: Let's go!

(They high five each other and exit)

ACT 3 SCENE 1

(Enter VIOLA, TOBY and ANDREW)

TOBY: *(To VIOLA)* Hello there! My niece, Olivia, would like to talk to you.

VIOLA: Well, that's why I'm here; I want to talk to her, too.

TOBY: Great! Taste your legs, sir. Put them to motion.

VIOLA: Taste your legs?

TOBY: Yeah. You know, hurry up. Don't you speak Shakespeare?

(Enter OLIVIA and MARIA)

VIOLA: Hi Olivia. Can I speak to you... *(Looks around at everybody)* in private?

OLIVIA: Of course. *(Clears her throat loudly; TOBY, ANDREW and MARIA exit)*

OLIVIA: What is your name, anyway?

VIOLA: Cesario. But I'm here to talk about...

OLIVIA: I know, I know. Orsino! Yuck. I beg you never speak again of him. Let's talk about me instead. *(Pause)* I love you. *(Uncomfortable silence)*

VIOLA: I pity you.

OLIVIA: *(To the audience)* I guess that's better than nothing. This is a bit embarrassing... OK, you can leave now!!!

VIOLA: Great! Bye!

OLIVIA: *(Grabs VIOLA)* No wait! Stay!

VIOLA: *(To audience)* Go! Stay! What is wrong with this lady?

OLIVIA: Could you just TRY to love me? A little bit? Please?

VIOLA: I swear to you that I will never love you. EVER. See ya later. *(VIOLA exits)*

OLIVIA: Bummer! *(Exits)*

ACT 3 SCENE 2

(Enter TOBY, ANDREW and FABIAN)

ANDREW: *(To TOBY)* Olivia is never going to notice me. I'm leaving town.

FABIAN: Wait! Maybe she's just trying to make you jealous.

TOBY: *(Belches)* That's it! She wants you to win her over. You know what would really impress her? A duel! You should totally challenge Cesario!

FABIAN: Sir Toby's right. There is no way but this, Sir Andrew. You've got to fight for her.

ANDREW: I'll do it! I'm going to go challenge Cesario right now! *(ANDREW exits)*

FABIAN: I can't believe he fell for that.

TOBY: I know. But it will never happen...he's too much of a chicken.

(Enter MARIA)

MARIA: Hey guys, come quick! Malvolio is wearing his hideous yellow stockings and smiling so much! I know my lady will strike him.

TOBY: Sweet, more entertainment! Come on! *(They exit)*

ACT 3 SCENE 3

(Enter SEBASTIAN and ANTONIO)

SEBASTIAN: Thanks for coming with me, Antonio. You're a great friend.

ANTONIO: No problem. Listen, want to find a hotel? In the south suburbs, we can stay at the Elephant hotel.

SEBASTIAN: The Elephant? But I didn't bring my trunk! Get it? Elephant? Trunk?

ANTONIO: *(Not laughing)* That was really bad.

SEBASTIAN: It wasn't THAT bad. Anyway, let's go see the sights first! I've never been to Ilyria.

ANTONIO: Sorry, my friend. During the war I stole a lot of their money. So if the wrong people see me here, I could be in a lot of trouble.

SEBASTIAN: Do not then walk too open.

ANTONIO: I'll be careful. But here's some money, go have fun.

SEBASTIAN: Okay. Thanks, Antonio. See you later at the Elephant. *(SEBASTIAN holds arm out in front of face like a trunk and trumpets like an elephant; ANTONIO looks at the audience and shakes head. They exit)*

ACT 3 SCENE 4

(Enter OLIVIA and MARIA)

OLIVIA: Hey, where's Malvolio? He is sad and civil, just what I need right now to take my mind off of Cesario.

MARIA: He's coming, but in very strange manner. He is sure possessed.

OLIVIA: What's wrong with him?

MARIA: I think he's gone crazy. Here he comes!

(Enter MALVOLIO)

MALVOLIO: *(To OLIVIA)* Sweet lady, ho ho!

OLIVIA: Why are you smiling? I want you to be sad.

MALVOLIO: *(Smiling)* I'm following your letter, see? *(Points to his yellow socks)* I'm seizing the day, Olivia! Carpe diem!

OLIVIA: You're right, Maria, he's obviously gone insane. Have my uncle Toby watch over Malvolio until he feels better. I hope he's not crazy forever.

(MARIA and OLIVIA exit)

MALVOLIO: *(To audience)* She must love me! She's having her uncle take care of me! This is SO great.

(Enter MARIA, TOBY and FABIAN)

FABIAN: How is't with you, Malvolio?

MALVOLIO: Leave me alone.

MARIA: Sir Toby, you're supposed to take care of him. Olivia said so.

TOBY: We need to be careful with him. I hear he's gone nuts! He might be dangerous!

(They all start backing away from MALVOLIO)

MALVOLIO: I don't have time for this. I'm leaving.

(MALVOLIO exits)

FABIAN: Why, we shall make him mad indeed.

MARIA: The house will be the quieter.

(Enter ANDREW)

FABIAN: *(To audience)* Speaking of crazy people...

ANDREW: Here's the challenge, read it.

TOBY: *(Reads letter)* "Cesario, I don't know you, but I really don't like you and I think we should duel. Sincerely, Sir Andrew."

FABIAN: *(Sarcastically)* Well, that should terrify him.

MARIA: And he just happens to be here in the other room with my lady, Olivia!

TOBY: Great! I'll deliver your letter. Go wait for him in the garden. As soon as you see him, attack him with your sword!

ANDREW: Got it! *(ANDREW exits)*

TOBY: I can't deliver this letter; it's...dumb. I will deliver his challenge by word of mouth.

(Enter VIOLA)

TOBY: Cesario! There's a pretty angry knight waiting for you outside. Thy assailant is quick, skillful and deadly, and wants to kill you.

VIOLA: What?! Somebody's mad at me? I didn't do anything!

TOBY: Come on, just go out and fight him! *(Pause)* I'll let him know you're coming! *(TOBY exits)*

FABIAN: Seriously, dude, the knight who wants to fight you is the most skillful, bloody and fatal opposite that you could have possibly found in any part of Illyria. *(Winks at audience)* Do you want me to go with you?

VIOLA: Yes, thank you. I hate fighting.

(VIOLA and FABIAN exit; Enter TOBY and ANDREW)

TOBY: You better prepare yourself. They say he is the best in this kingdom!

ANDREW: Uh-oh. I'll not meddle with him.

TOBY: I don't think you can get out of it now. Here they come!

(Enter VIOLA and FABIAN)

FABIAN: LET'S DO THIS!!

(VIOLA and ANDREW pull out their swords and start walking towards each other with their eyes closed; Enter ANTONIO)

ANTONIO: Stop! Put up your sword.

TOBY: Who in the heck are you?

ANTONIO: I'm his friend *(Points to VIOLA)*. I'd do anything for him!

TOBY and VIOLA: Huh?

TOBY: Well then, let's fight! *(He pulls out a sword)*

(Enter POLICEMAN)

POLICEMAN: *(Grabs ANTONIO)* This is the man! You are under arrest for stealing our money! Let's go!

ANTONIO: *(To VIOLA)* See, I told you they don't like me. Listen, do you still have that money I gave you?

VIOLA: What money, sir? I have no idea who you are!

ANTONIO: Seriously? You're going to pretend not to know me? This is ridiculous! *(To the POLICEMAN)* You see, I rescued him when he was drowning and have really been a good friend to him.

POLICEMAN: Waa, waa, waa.

ANTONIO: *(To VIOLA)* Thanks a lot, Sebastian.

(POLICEMAN takes ANTONIO away)

VIOLA: *(To audience)* Wow. He was really upset. He nam'd Sebastian, my brother's name? Is he alive?! How cool would that be! *(VIOLA exits)*

TOBY: I can't believe Cesario just let his friend be taken away like that!

ANDREW: I know! Now I really want to go beat him up!

FABIAN: Well, what are we waiting for? Let's go get him!

(All exit)

ACT 4 SCENE 1

(Enter SEBASTIAN, ANDREW, TOBY and FABIAN)

ANDREW: *(To SEBASTIAN)* Ah-HA! I knew I'd find you, Cesario! *(ANDREW draws his sword and pokes SEBASTIAN)* There's for you.

SEBASTIAN: *(Pulls his sword and begins fighting with ANDREW)* Why there's for thee, and there, and there! Holy cow! Is everyone in Ilyria crazy? I swear I don't know any of you people!

(TOBY sneaks up and grabs SEBASTIAN from behind)

TOBY: Gotcha!

SEBASTIAN: Let me go! This is SO not cool!

TOBY: *(Belches in SEBASTIAN'S ear)* No way, José.

(SEBASTIAN breaks free and TOBY draws his sword; FABIAN hides behind ANDREW; Enter OLIVIA)

OLIVIA: Stop this right now! Uncle Toby, leave poor Cesario alone and get out of my sight!

TOBY: Sorry, Olivia.

(TOBY, ANDREW and FABIAN exit)

OLIVIA: Those boys are so childish with all their fighting. Why don't you come back to my house for a while?

SEBASTIAN: *(To audience)* She called me "Cesario" too, but she's really cute, so I think I'll go with her. *(To OLIVIA)* Madam, I will. *(They exit)*

ACT 4 SCENE 2

(Enter CLOWN and MALVOLIO. MALVOLIO'S hands are tied and he is blindfolded)

CLOWN: What's up, crazy guy?

MALVOLIO: Is that you, Clown? Can you help me?

CLOWN: Sorry, I don't help crazy people.

MALVOLIO: I'm not crazy, you fool! Sir Toby tied me up! *(Starts crying like a baby)* I want my mommy!

CLOWN: *(To Audience)* Well, this is embarrassing. *(To MALVOLIO)* Okay, okay, I'll help you. But tell me true, are you not mad indeed?

MALVOLIO: *(Still crying)* Believe me, I am not. I tell thee true. Waaaaaaa!

CLOWN: *(Unties MALVOLIO and removes blindfold)* ALRIGHT! Look, Maria, Sir Toby and Sir Andrew played a joke on you. Olivia never wrote that letter.

MALVOLIO: WHAT?! I'll be revenged on the whole pack of them! They have done me wrong!

(MALVOLIO storms off stage in a rage; CLOWN shrugs his shoulders)

CLOWN: *(To audience)* I must admit, it was kind of funny!

ACT 4 SCENE 3

(Enter SEBASTIAN)

SEBASTIAN: This is the air, that is the glorious sun. This MUST be a dream! WOW, Olivia loves me! I don't even care that she keeps calling me Cesario and I met her this morning!

(Enter OLIVIA)

OLIVIA: I don't mean to rush you, Cesario, but I found a priest who agreed to marry us...now. What do you say?

SEBASTIAN: Sure, why not? Let's get married! Lead the way to the good father!

(They exit very excited and high fiving)

ACT 5 SCENE 1

(Enter ORSINO, VIOLA, and other LORDS if needed)

ORSINO: Today's the day, Cesario! Olivia will finally realize that I'm the man for her.

VIOLA: Hey look! There's the guy who got dragged away by the police!

(Enter ANTONIO and POLICEMAN)

ORSINO: That face of his I do remember well. Hey, you stole our money!

POLICEMAN: Yeah, he's a stinky pirate.

ANTONIO: I am not a pirate, and I am not stinky! I'm only here because I rescued HIM from drowning *(Points to VIOLA)*, and now he's pretending that he doesn't know who I am! *(Whines)* And he was my best friend.

ORSINO: When came he to this town?

ANTONIO: Got here this morning.

ORSINO: This morning! Then you really have lost your mind. Cesario's been serving me for three months!

(Enter OLIVIA)

OLIVIA: Orsino, you're here again?! I. Don't. Like. You. Okay?

ORSINO: Still so cruel?

OLIVIA: Still so constant, lord.

ORSINO: Fine then, I'm leaving. Come on, Cesario.

OLIVIA: Where do you think you're going, Cesario?!

VIOLA: With Orsino. I love him.

ORSINO: Let's go, Cesario!

OLIVIA: Cesario, husband, stay!

VIOLA: *(Whispers)* Husband?

ORSINO and CURIO: Husband?!

OLIVIA: Yes, HUSBAND! Cesario and I were married earlier today.

(Enter ANDREW, TOBY and CLOWN, all moaning and covered in bandages)

ANDREW: AH! My head! *(Grabs head)*

TOBY: AH! My leg!! *(Grabs leg and belches)*

CLOWN: *(Sarcastically)* AH! My brain!

OLIVIA: Who did this to you?

ANDREW: Cesario! We took him for a coward, but he's the very devil incardinate. *(Points to VIOLA)* There he is!

VIOLA: What are you talking about? I never hurt you.

TOBY: Are you kidding me? You just bashed him in the head!

OLIVIA: Enough! Fool, get him to bed, and let his hurt be looked to. All of you! Go!

(Exit TOBY, ANDREW and CLOWN; CLOWN reenters after pushing TOBY & ANDREW offstage; enter SEBASTIAN)

SEBASTIAN: *(To OLIVIA)* Sorry I'm late, dear wife, but I got into a fight with your uncle. *(Notices ANTONIO)* Antonio! Hey buddy! Where on earth have you been?

(Everyone looks at SEBASTIAN, then at VIOLA, then at SEBASTIAN again)

ORSINO: One face, one voice, one habit, and two persons!

ANTONIO: Um...if you're Sebastian, then who is THAT? *(Points at VIOLA)*

SEBASTIAN: Do I stand there? I never had a brother. I had a sister, but she drowned.

VIOLA: No she didn't! *(Takes off her disguise)* It's me!

SEBASTIAN: Viola! Sister!

(They run to each other and perform a long, elaborate secret handshake).

OLIVIA and ORSINO: You're a GIRL?

VIOLA: One hundred percent!

SEBASTIAN: *(To OLIVIA)* See! It all worked out. You fell in love with my sister, but in the end you got me! *(Laughs)*

(Everyone except VIOLA starts laughing)

ORSINO: *(To VIOLA)* It's okay, Cesario, er, I mean...Viola, I think you're super cute! So cute, that I want to marry you!

VIOLA: Yes! Score!

ORSINO: Indeed!

CLOWN: Let the celebrating begin! *(Begins to sing a popular love song; Everyone on stage begins to dance to CLOWN'S song, dancing their way off the stage.)*

THE END

The 20-Minute or so Twelfth Night

By William Shakespeare
Creatively modified by Brendan P. Kelso and Khara C. Oliver

15-20+ Actors
CAST OF CHARACTERS:

ORSINO: a duke, loves Olivia

VIOLA: girl pretending to be a boy named, Cesario

SEBASTIAN: Viola's twin brother (they look alike!)

LADY OLIVIA: loves Cesario (that's Viola. Confused yet?)

SIR TOBY BELCH: uncle to Olivia (likes to burp!)

*SIR ANDREW: friend to Toby; likes Olivia

MARIA: lady in waiting (for what, we are not sure)

THE CLOWN: funny guy (a fool)

**MALVOLIO: Olivia's servant with funny socks

FABIAN: Olivia's other servant

ANTONIO: Sebastian's friend, enemy of Orsino

VALENTINE: Orsino's servant

CURIO: Orsino's other servant

*SEA CAPTAIN: a sea captain

SAILORS: they sail

***PRIEST: he marries people and wears a cool robe

**POLICEMAN #1: 1st policeman

***POLICEMAN #2: 2nd policeman

**MUSICIAN(S): they play music (if needed)

***SERVANT: a servant, with on short line

PlayingWithPlays.com

47

LORDS and **LADIES** of the court (if needed)

*The same actor can play Sea Captain and Sir Andrew
**The same actor can play Malvolio, Police #1, and Musician
***The same actor can play the Priest, Police #2, Servant and another Musician

PROLOGUE

(Enter VIOLA and SEBASTIAN, wearing identical clothes so the audience knows they are twins)

SEBASTIAN: *(To audience with VIOLA standing next to him)* She is my twin sister.

VIOLA: He is my twin brother.

SEBASTIAN: Enjoy the show! *(All exit)*

ACT 1 SCENE 1

(Enter ORSINO, CURIO, other LORDS and MUSICIANS)

ORSINO: If music be the food of love, play on! *(ORSINO looks depressed)*

MUSICIANS: La, la la la la.... *(while dancing a bit crazy, then exit)*

CURIO: What would make you feel better, my lord Orsino?

ORSINO: The most beautiful lady of the land! *(Talking to a picture of Olivia he is holding)* Oh, Olivia...why won't you notice me? Why?

(CURIO rolls eyes and shakes head; enter VALENTINE)

ORSINO: How now, what news from her?

VALENTINE: Sorry, man. Olivia's brother just died, and she is so bummed, that she decided to hide and cry for the next seven years.

ORSINO: Seven years? Are you sure you don't mean seven days, or maybe even seven months?

VALENTINE: Nope, SEVEN YEARS!

ORSINO: Seriously? Wow! *(To audience)* You have to admire that kind of dedication. I think I love her even more now. *(Sighs again; all exit)*

ACT 1 SCENE 2

(Enter VIOLA, SEA CAPTAIN and SAILORS)

VIOLA: Whew! What a terrible shipwreck!

SAILOR: That totally stunk!

(Other sailors agree with him. One sailor acts REALLY seasick)

VIOLA: O my poor twin brother, Sebastian, may have drowned. *(To Sea Captain)* Captain, do you think there's any chance he made it?

SEA CAPTAIN: Could be, Viola, let's stay optimistic.

VIOLA: Where are we?

SEA CAPTAIN: This is Illyria, lady, ruled by the noble Duke Orsino.

VIOLA: Hmmm...I remember hearing that he was single and cute!

SEA CAPTAIN: Yes, but he is in love with the fair Olivia.

VIOLA: *(To audience)* Hey! I'm going to disguise myself like a man, and I'll serve this duke. He'll like me 'cause I'm a really good singer. *(Singing in a really low voice)* Row, row, row your boat...

SEA CAPTAIN: Sure! *(Covering his ears because it sounds so bad)* But, ahhh, do me a favor, don't sing... just do the disguise thing. TRUST ME! *(All exit)*

ACT 1 SCENE 3

(Enter SIR TOBY BELCH, MARIA and SIR ANDREW)

TOBY: *(Belches)* Maria, what is with my niece Olivia? She

PlayingWithPlays.com

49

is taking this "mourning" thing waaaaay too seriously. Being so sad all the time is not good for your health.

MARIA: Gross, quit belching Sir Toby BELCH.

ANDREW: He can't help it if that's his name! Sir Toby Belch!

TOBY: That's right, sweet Sir Andrew!

MARIA: Whatever. Look you two, why don't you just get on with your night of silliness? I have better things to do.

(MARIA exits)

ANDREW: Since your niece, Olivia, is being such a bummer, I'll ride home tomorrow, Sir Toby.

TOBY: Pourquoi, my dear knight?

ANDREW: What is "pourquoi"?

TOBY: Poor-kwah means "why" in French. Makes me sound smart, doesn't it?

ANDREW: Oh, I wish I had paid more attention in school!

TOBY: Andrew, please stay. Olivia could snap out of it, and who knows, she might actually think you're cute. *(Shakes head at audience)*

ANDREW: Oh, alright, I'll stay a month longer. But let's go dancing! I'm a really good dancer. *(He starts to dance like a crazy man)*

TOBY: *(Pumps his fist in the air)* Sir Andrew in the HOUSE! Go Andy! Go Andy! Go! Go! Go Andy!

(All exit dancing)

ACT 1 SCENE 4

(Enter VALENTINE and VIOLA dressed as a man "Cesario")

VALENTINE: Cesario!

VIOLA: *(In a fake man-voice and winks at audience)* Yes?

VALENTINE: Listen, the duke Orsino thinks you're cool.

VIOLA: Really? I thank you. Here comes the count now.

(Enter ORSINO)

ORSINO: Cesario! Go tell Olivia how much I like her, no... LOVE her....Be not denied access, stand at her doors, and stay there till she talks to you.

VIOLA: Orsino, what happened to seven years? 1, 2, 3....

ORSINO: Ugh! Seven, schmevin! *(Stamps foot)*. I don't care. Be clamorous. Be loud. Be rude. Just don't take no for an answer!

VIOLA: When I see her, what then?

ORSINO: Tell her I love her. Act like me and say smart things.

VIOLA: And you can't go because....

ORSINO: 'Cause I'm a duke! I don't do anything for myself. *(Snaps his fingers at VALENTINE and points to his untied shoe. VALENTINE hurries to tie it)* And you're soooo *(Confused suddenly)* pretty? Er...handsome. *(Starts looking funny at VIOLA)* Just go!

VIOLA: Fine, fine. I'll do my best to woo your lady. *(To audience pointing at ORSINO)* But it's going to be so hard! Because after these last three days of tying his shoes, I TOTALLY want to marry him myself! *(All exit)*

ACT 1 SCENE 5

(Enter MARIA and CLOWN)

CLOWN: Those that are fools, let them use their talents.

MARIA: What?

CLOWN: You know, "fool" another name for a clown.... *(With two thumbs pointed at himself)*

MARIA: You are so silly; here comes my lady, Olivia.

(Enter OLIVIA, and ATTENDANTS)

OLIVIA: *(Using air quotes)* Go away, Clown, take the "fool" away.

CLOWN: But I can make you laugh! *(Makes a silly face)* And you need to laugh because you're acting so sad...give me another chance, pretty please? *(Falls on ground and pretends to cry)*

(ATTENDANTS laugh and point at CLOWN)

CLOWN: See, I'm funny!

OLIVIA: Yes, but you are funnier off stage, now go.

CLOWN: BORING....

(Exit CLOWN, MARIA and ATTENDANTS; enter MALVOLIO)

MALVOLIO: Lady Olivia, there is at the gate a young gentleman who much desires to speak with you.

OLIVIA: Nope.

MALVOLIO: Seriously, I told him you were sick. I told him you were asleep. I told him you were sick in your sleep. The dude is NOT leaving.

OLIVIA: Fine. Let him approach.

(Throws a blanket over her head)

(MALVOLIO exits; Enter VIOLA disguised as Cesario)

VIOLA: Um, hi. Are you Olivia?

OLIVIA: Maybe.

VIOLA: Well I heard Olivia is the most radiant, exquisite, and unmatchable beauty, like, EVER.

OLIVIA: That would be me.

VIOLA: *(To audience)* Now we're getting somewhere. *(To OLIVIA)* AHEM: Orsino loves you with all of his heart.

OLIVIA: Are you a comedian? *(Takes off blanket)*

VIOLA: Wow, you are pretty.

OLIVIA: I know.

VIOLA: I see you what you are, you are too proud.

OLIVIA: Look, I know Orsino is young, noble, and rich, but I cannot love him.

VIOLA: *(To audience)* Well, I don't get it, but hey, I tried. Farewell, fair cruelty! *(VIOLA exits)*

OLIVIA: *(To audience)* OMG! Isn't he perfect!? Oh, I am so in L-O-V-E with that boy! *(Yells off stage)* Malvolio!

(Enter MALVOLIO)

OLIVIA: Run after him and tell him he has to come back tomorrow!

(MALVOLIO exits, OLIVIA skips off stage giggling)

ACT 2 SCENE 1

(Enter ANTONIO and SEBASTIAN)

SEBASTIAN: Thanks for saving my life Antonio. Gotta go, see ya later!

ANTONIO: Whoa, Sebastian. Can I go with you? You're my new best friend!

SEBASTIAN: Nah. I am a really bummed that my twin sister, Viola, drowned some hour before you found me.

ANTONIO: That's awful. You really shouldn't be alone. Let me be your servant.

SEBASTIAN: Sure, that sounds cool, come on! *(All exit)*

ACT 2 SCENE 2

(Enter VIOLA with MALVOLIO following behind)

MALVOLIO: Excuse me, sir! Wait up!

VIOLA: Yes?

MALVOLIO: Olivia says you HAVE to come back tomorrow.

VIOLA: I really don't want to.

MALVOLIO: Well, I don't think you really have a choice. See ya!

(MALVOLIO exits)

VIOLA: *(To audience)* Uh-oh. I think Olivia has a crush on me. This is getting confusing. So, let's review: I'm in love with Orsino *(ORSINO pops his head out from offstage and waves at audience),* he's in love with Olivia *(OLIVIA pops her head out from offstage and waves at audience),* and she's in love with me! O time, thou must untangle this, not I, it is too hard a knot for me to untie! *(In a whisper voice)* that means only time will fix this! *(Exits)*

ACT 2 SCENE 3

(Enter SIR TOBY BELCH and SIR ANDREW having a belching contest, and CLOWN follows)

CLOWN: STOP THAT!!! It's disgusting!

TOBY: *(Belches and smiles at CLOWN)* What a great party! Let's stay up the rest of the night and celebrate!

ANDREW: Our lives consist of eating and drinking! To be up late is to be up late! *(Belches to Clown)*

CLOWN: You guys are SOOOO gross!

(Enter MARIA)

MARIA: It's three in the morning! If you guys don't keep it quiet, Olivia will send Malvolio to yell at you.

TOBY: *(Sarcastically)* Oh no! Not Malvolio! *(Belches, and shoots a quick glance at CLOWN)*

(Enter MALVOLIO)

TOBY & ANDREW: *(To audience)* Uh-oh, Malvolio!

54

MALVOLIO: I should have known it was you fools making all this racket. Have you no wit, manners, nor honesty, but to gabble like tinkers at this time of night?

ANDREW: Oh, puh-lease...What does "gabble" mean anyway?

MALVOLIO: To talk...

CLOWN: And belch!

MALVOLIO: ...and talk...on, and on, and on... Look, Toby, Olivia told me that if you don't start acting like a proper gentleman, she is very willing to bid you farewell; even if you are her uncle.

TOBY: Oh, I'm soooo scared! Listen, you goody-two-shoes, leave us alone.

MALVOLIO: You people are hopeless.

(MALVOLIO exits)

ANDREW: What a fuddy-duddy.

MARIA: Listen guys, I have an evil plan! Let's play a joke on Malvolio!

TOBY: What wilt thou do?

MARIA: I will write a romantic letter from Olivia about how she's in love with Malvolio. He'll believe it and when he finds out the truth, he'll feel like a total blockhead.

ANDREW: Brilliant! You are a genius, Maria!

(All exit; TOBY and ANDREW start belching again)

ACT 2 SCENE 4

(Enter ORSINO, and VIOLA)

ORSINO: Let me tell you something, Cesario, if ever thou shalt love, you will finally know what it's like to be me right now. All I can think of is Olivia. Olivia, Olivia, Olivia! *(Sighs* *and looks at VIOLA and pauses for effect)* My gut tells me you've fallen in love with someone, am I right?

VIOLA: *(Surprised)* Well, kind of. *(To audience, VIOLA starts pointing at ORSINO)*

ORSINO: That's great! What kind of girl is she?

VIOLA: *(Glancing at the audience)* She's, um, like you.

ORSINO: She is not worth thee, then. How old is she?

VIOLA: *(Still looking at the audience)* About your years, my lord. *(To the audience)* and size, height, weight...smell....

ORSINO: Too old, by heaven! Enough about you, let's talk about me. Where were we, oh yes! Olivia!!! Go and tell her I care only for her.

VIOLA: Sorry, Orsino, but she really doesn't love you. I don't even think she LIKES you.

ORSINO: I will make her love me. I know I can.

VIOLA: *(Sighs)* If you say so. Sir, shall I to this lady, Olivia?

ORSINO: Yes! And give her this jewel.

VIOLA: Right! Off I go! *(All exit)*

ACT 2 SCENE 5

(Enter TOBY, ANDREW and FABIAN)

TOBY: Come on Fabian, let's watch Malvolio's reaction to "the love letter."

FABIAN: I wouldn't miss this for the world!

(Enter MARIA)

MARIA: Hide! Here comes Malvolio! *(She tosses a letter on the ground; MARIA exits, the men "hide" upstage; Enter MALVOLIO)*

MALVOLIO: I am feeling very lucky today. What's this? *(Picks up letter and opens it)* Why, it's a letter from Olivia! I wonder who it's for? *(Reads)* "Jove knows I love, but who?" Sounds very Shakespearean.

ANDREW: Can you believe this guy?

FABIAN: Shhhh! This is good stuff!

MALVOLIO:*(Reads)* "Malvolio, I don't care if you're my servant. Some are born great, some achieve greatness, and some have greatness thrust upon 'em. Please wear those ridiculous yellow stockings that I love. I love you!" Woo-hoo! Oh, I am so happy! She loves me! Oh, to be Count Malvolio!

(MALVOLIO exits dancing and singing; TOBY, ANDREW and FABIAN laugh)

TOBY: Seriously, I could marry Maria for her brilliance.

ANDREW: So could I too!

FABIAN: So could I three!

(Enter MARIA)

MARIA: Does it work upon him?

TOBY: Does it work upon him? If you mean, how did it go, it was amazing. He believed every word!

MARIA: Cool! He'll come to her in those ugly yellow stockings that she hates, and she'll be totally annoyed by his happiness.

ANDREW: Let's go!

(They high five each other and exit)

ACT 3 SCENE 1

(Enter VIOLA, TOBY and ANDREW)

TOBY: *(To VIOLA)* Hello there! My niece, Olivia, would like to talk to you.

VIOLA: Well, that's why I'm here; I want to talk to her, too.

TOBY: Great! Taste your legs, sir. Put them to motion.

VIOLA: Taste your legs?

TOBY: Yeah. You know, hurry up. Don't you speak Shakespeare?

(Enter OLIVIA and MARIA)

VIOLA: Hi Olivia. Can I speak to you... *(Looks around at everybody)* in private?

OLIVIA: Of course. *(Clears her throat loudly; TOBY, ANDREW and MARIA exit)*

OLIVIA: What is your name, anyway?

VIOLA: Cesario. But I'm here to talk about...

OLIVIA: I know, I know. Orsino! Yuck. I beg you never speak again of him. Let's talk about me instead. *(Pause)* I love you. *(Uncomfortable silence)*

VIOLA: I pity you.

OLIVIA: *(To the audience)* I guess that's better than nothing. This is a bit embarrassing... OK, you can leave now!!!

VIOLA: Great! Bye!

OLIVIA: *(Grabs VIOLA)* No wait! Stay!

VIOLA: *(To audience)* Go! Stay! What is wrong with this lady?

OLIVIA: Could you just TRY to love me? A little bit? Please?

VIOLA: I swear to you that I will never love you. EVER. See ya later. *(VIOLA exits)*

OLIVIA: Bummer! *(Exits)*

ACT 3 SCENE 2

(Enter TOBY, ANDREW and FABIAN)

ANDREW: *(To TOBY)* Olivia is never going to notice me. I'm leaving town.

FABIAN: Wait! Maybe she's just trying to make you jealous.

TOBY: *(Belches)* That's it! She wants you to win her over. You know what would really impress her? A duel! You should totally challenge Cesario!

FABIAN: Sir Toby's right. There is no way but this, Sir Andrew. You've got to fight for her.

ANDREW: I'll do it! I'm going to go challenge Cesario right now!

(ANDREW exits)

FABIAN: I can't believe he fell for that.

TOBY: I know. But it will never happen...he's too much of a chicken.

(Enter MARIA)

MARIA: Hey guys, come quick! Malvolio is wearing his hideous yellow stockings and smiling so much! I know my lady will strike him.

TOBY: Sweet, more entertainment! Come on!

(They exit)

ACT 3 SCENE 3

(Enter SEBASTIAN and ANTONIO)

SEBASTIAN: Thanks for coming with me, Antonio. You're a great friend.

ANTONIO: No problem. Listen, want to find a hotel? In the south suburbs, we can stay at the Elephant hotel.

SEBASTIAN: The Elephant? But I didn't bring my trunk! Get it? Elephant? Trunk?

ANTONIO: *(Not laughing)* That was really bad.

SEBASTIAN: It wasn't THAT bad. Anyway, let's go see the sights first! I've never been to Ilyria.

ANTONIO: Sorry, my friend. During the war I stole a lot of their money. So if the wrong people see me here, I could be in a lot of trouble.

SEBASTIAN: Do not then walk too open.

ANTONIO: I'll be careful. But here's some money, go have fun.

SEBASTIAN: Okay. Thanks, Antonio. See you later at the Elephant. *(SEBASTIAN holds arm out in front of face like a trunk and trumpets like an elephant; ANTONIO looks at the audience and shakes head. They exit)*

ACT 3 SCENE 4

(Enter OLIVIA and MARIA)

OLIVIA: Hey, where's Malvolio? He is sad and civil, just what I need right now to take my mind off of Cesario.

MARIA: He's coming, but in very strange manner. He is sure possessed.

OLIVIA: What's wrong with him?

MARIA: I think he's gone crazy. Here he comes!

(Enter MALVOLIO)

MALVOLIO: *(To OLIVIA)* Sweet lady, ho ho!

OLIVIA: Why are you smiling? I want you to be sad.

MALVOLIO: *(Smiling)* I'm following your letter, see? *(Points to his yellow socks)* I'm seizing the day, Olivia! Carpe diem!

OLIVIA: You're right, Maria, he's obviously gone insane.

60   PlayingWithPlays.com

SERVANT: Lady Olivia, the young gentleman, Cesario came back and he's waiting for you. *(SERVANT exits)*

OLIVIA: Tell him I'll be right there. *(To MARIA)* Have my uncle Toby watch over Malvolio until he feels better. I hope he's not crazy forever.

(MARIA and OLIVIA exit)

MALVOLIO: *(To audience)* She must love me! She's having her uncle take care of me! This is SO great.

(Enter MARIA, TOBY and FABIAN)

FABIAN: How is't with you, Malvolio?

MALVOLIO: Leave me alone.

MARIA: Sir Toby, you're supposed to take care of him. Olivia said so.

TOBY: We need to be careful with him. I hear he's gone nuts! He might be dangerous!

(They all start backing away from MALVOLIO)

MALVOLIO: I don't have time for this. I'm leaving.

(MALVOLIO exits)

FABIAN: Why, we shall make him mad indeed.

MARIA: The house will be the quieter.

(Enter ANDREW)

FABIAN: *(To audience)* Speaking of crazy people...

ANDREW: Here's the challenge, read it.

TOBY: *(Reads letter)* "Cesario, I don't know you, but I really don't like you and I think we should duel. Sincerely, Sir Andrew"

FABIAN: *(Sarcastically)* Well, that should terrify him.

MARIA: And he just happens to be here in the other room with my lady, Olivia!

TOBY: Great! I'll deliver your letter. Go wait for him in the garden. As soon as you see him, attack him with your sword!

ANDREW: Got it! *(ANDREW exits)*

TOBY: I can't deliver this letter; it's...dumb. I will deliver his challenge by word of mouth.

(Enter VIOLA)

TOBY: Cesario! There's a pretty angry knight waiting for you outside. Thy assailant is quick, skillful and deadly, and wants to kill you.

VIOLA: What?! Somebody's mad at me? I didn't do anything!

TOBY: Come on, just go out and fight him! *(Pause)* I'll let him know you're coming! *(TOBY exits)*

FABIAN: Seriously, dude, the knight who wants to fight you is the most skillful, bloody and fatal opposite that you could have possibly found in any part of Illyria. *(Winks at audience)* Do you want me to go with you?

VIOLA: Yes, thank you. I hate fighting.

(VIOLA and FABIAN exit; Enter TOBY and ANDREW)

TOBY: You better prepare yourself. They say he is the best in this kingdom!

ANDREW: Uh-oh. I'll not meddle with him.

TOBY: I don't think you can get out of it now. Here they come!

(Enter VIOLA and FABIAN)

FABIAN: LET'S DO THIS!!

(VIOLA and ANDREW pull out their swords and start walking towards each other with their eyes closed; Enter ANTONIO)

ANTONIO: Stop! Put up your sword.

TOBY: Who in the heck are you?

ANTONIO: I'm his friend *(Points to VIOLA).* I'd do anything for him!

TOBY and VIOLA: Huh?

TOBY: Well then, let's fight! *(He pulls out a sword)*

(Enter POLICE)

POLICEMAN #1: This is the man, grab him!

POLICEMAN #2: *(Grabs ANTONIO)* You are under arrest for stealing our money! Let's go!

ANTONIO: *(To VIOLA)* See, I told you they don't like me. Listen, do you still have that money I gave you?

VIOLA: What money, sir? I have no idea who you are!

ANTONIO: Seriously? You're going to pretend not to know me? This is ridiculous! *(To the POLICEMAN)* You see, I rescued him when he was drowning and have really been a good friend to him.

POLICEMAN #1: Waa, waa, waa.

ANTONIO: *(To VIOLA)* Thanks a lot, Sebastian.

(POLICEMEN take ANTONIO away)

VIOLA: *(To audience)* Wow. He was really upset. He nam'd Sebastian, my brother's name? Is he alive?! How cool would that be! *(VIOLA exits)*

TOBY: I can't believe Cesario just let his friend be taken away like that!

PlayingWithPlays.com

63

ANDREW: I know! Now I really want to go beat him up!

FABIAN: Well, what are we waiting for? Let's go get him!

(All exit)

ACT 4 SCENE 1

(Enter SEBASTIAN, ANDREW, TOBY and FABIAN)

ANDREW: *(To SEBASTIAN)* Ah-HA! I knew I'd find you, Cesario! *(ANDREW draws his sword and pokes SEBASTIAN)* There's for you.

SEBASTIAN: *(Pulls his sword and begins fighting with ANDREW)* Why there's for thee, and there, and there! Holy cow! Is everyone in Ilyria crazy? I swear I don't know any of you people!

(TOBY sneaks up and grabs SEBASTIAN from behind)

TOBY: Gotcha!

SEBASTIAN: Let me go! This is SO not cool!

TOBY: *(Belches in SEBASTIAN'S ear)* No way, José.

(SEBASTIAN breaks free and TOBY draws his sword; FABIAN hides behind ANDREW; Enter OLIVIA)

OLIVIA: Stop this right now! Uncle Toby, leave poor Cesario alone and get out of my sight!

TOBY: Sorry, Olivia.

(TOBY, ANDREW and FABIAN exit)

OLIVIA: Those boys are so childish with all their fighting. Why don't you come back to my house for a while?

SEBASTIAN: *(To audience)* She called me "Cesario" too, but she's really cute, so I think I'll go with her. *(To OLIVIA)* Madam, I will. *(They exit)*

ACT 4 SCENE 2

(Enter CLOWN and MALVOLIO. MALVOLIO'S hands are tied and he is blindfolded)

CLOWN: What's up, crazy guy?

MALVOLIO: Is that you, Clown? Can you help me?

CLOWN: Sorry, I don't help crazy people.

MALVOLIO: I'm not crazy, you fool! Sir Toby tied me up! *(Starts crying like a baby)* I want my mommy!

CLOWN: *(To Audience)* Well, this is embarrassing. *(To MALVOLIO)* Okay, okay, I'll help you. But tell me true, are you not mad indeed?

MALVOLIO: *(Still crying)* Believe me, I am not. I tell thee true. Waaaaaaa!

CLOWN: *(Unties MALVOLIO and removes blindfold)* ALRIGHT! Look, Maria, Sir Toby and Sir Andrew played a joke on you. Olivia never wrote that letter.

MALVOLIO: WHAT?! I'll be revenged on the whole pack of them! They have done me wrong!

(MALVOLIO storms off stage in a rage; CLOWN shrugs his shoulders)

CLOWN: *(To audience)* I must admit, it was kind of funny!

ACT 4 SCENE 3

(Enter SEBASTIAN)

SEBASTIAN: This is the air, that is the glorious sun. This MUST be a dream! WOW, Olivia loves me! I don't even care that she keeps calling me Cesario and I met her this morning!

(Enter OLIVIA and PRIEST)

OLIVIA: I don't mean to rush you, Cesario, but this priest has agreed to marry us...now. What do you say?

SEBASTIAN: Sure, why not?

OLIVIA: *(To PRIEST)* Lead the way, good father!

PRIEST: Okay. Do you?

SEBASTIAN: Yep!

PRIEST: Do you?

OLIVIA: You betcha!

PRIEST: Ok then, you're married!

(They all exit very excited high fiving)

ACT 5 SCENE 1

(Enter ORSINO, VIOLA, CURIO and other lords)

ORSINO: Today's the day, Cesario! Olivia will finally realize that I'm the man for her.

CURIO: *(Sarcastically)* I'm sure she will, Orsino.

VIOLA: Hey look! There's the guy who got dragged away by the police!

(Enter ANTONIO and POLICEMEN)

ORSINO: That face of his I do remember well. Hey, you stole our money!

POLICEMAN: Yeah, he's a stinky pirate.

ANTONIO: I am not a pirate, and I am not stinky! I'm only here because I rescued HIM from drowning *(Points to VIOLA)*, and now he's pretending that he doesn't know who I am! *(Whines)* And he was my best friend.

ORSINO: When came he to this town?

ANTONIO: Got here this morning.

ORSINO: This morning! Then you really have lost your mind. Cesario's been serving me for three months!

(Enter OLIVIA and LADIES)

OLIVIA: Orsino, you're here again?! I. Don't. Like. You. Okay?

ORSINO: Still so cruel?

OLIVIA: Still so constant, lord.

ORSINO: Fine then, I'm leaving. Come on, Cesario.

OLIVIA: Where do you think you're going, Cesario?!

VIOLA: With Orsino. I love him.

ORSINO: Let's go, Cesario!

OLIVIA: Cesario, husband, stay!

VIOLA: *(Whispers)* Husband?

ORSINO and CURIO: Husband?!

(Enter PRIEST)

PRIEST: Yes, HUSBAND. I married Olivia and Cesario earlier today.

(Enter ANDREW, TOBY and CLOWN, all moaning and covered in bandages)

ANDREW: AH! My head! *(Grabs head)*

TOBY: AH! My leg!! *(Grabs leg and belches)*

CLOWN: *(Sarcastically)* AH! My brain!

OLIVIA: Who did this to you?

ANDREW: Cesario! We took him for a coward, but he's the very devil incardinate. *(Points to VIOLA)* There he is!

VIOLA: What are you talking about? I never hurt you.

TOBY: Are you kidding me? You just bashed him in the head!

OLIVIA: Enough! Fool, get him to bed, and let his hurt be looked to. All of you! Go!

(Exit TOBY, ANDREW and CLOWN; CLOWN reenters after pushing TOBY & ANDREW offstage; enter SEBASTIAN)

SEBASTIAN: *(To OLIVIA)* Sorry I'm late, dear wife, but I got into a fight with your uncle. *(Notices ANTONIO)* Antonio! Hey buddy! Where on earth have you been?

(Everyone looks at SEBASTIAN, then at VIOLA, then at SEBASTIAN again)

ORSINO: One face, one voice, one habit, and two persons!

ANTONIO: Um...if you're Sebastian, then who is THAT? *(Points at VIOLA)*

SEBASTIAN: Do I stand there? I never had a brother. I had a sister, but she drowned.

VIOLA: No she didn't! *(Takes off her disguise)* It's me!

SEBASTIAN: Viola! Sister!

(They run to each other and perform a long, elaborate secret handshake).

OLIVIA and ORSINO: You're a GIRL?

VIOLA: One hundred percent!

SEBASTIAN: *(To OLIVIA)* See! It all worked out. You fell in love with my sister, but in the end you got me! *(Laughs)*

(Everyone except VIOLA starts laughing)

ORSINO: *(To VIOLA)* It's okay, Cesario, er, I mean...Viola, I think you're super cute! So cute, that I want to marry you!

VIOLA: Yes! Score!

ORSINO: Indeed!

CLOWN: Let the celebrating begin! *(Begins to sing a popular love song; Everyone on stage begins to dance to CLOWN'S song, dancing their way off the stage.)*

THE END

ABOUT THE AUTHORS

BRENDAN P. KELSO, known to the kids as Professor Peculiar because of his unique and humorous personality, came to writing modified Shakespeare scripts when he was taking time off from work to be at home with his son. "It just grew from there". Within months, he was being asked to offer classes in various locations and acting organizations along the coast of California. Employed as an engineer, Brendan never thought about writing. But, he has always believed, "the best way to learn is to have fun!" Brendan makes his home on the central coast of California and loves to spend time with his wife and son.

KHARA C. OLIVER first fell in love with Shakespeare in 8th grade after reading Hamlet, and she has been an avid fan ever since. She studied Shakespeare's works in Stratford-upon-Avon, and graduated with a degree in English from UCLA. Khara is lucky to have a terrific career and a charmed life on the Central Coast of CA, but what she cherishes most is time spent with her husband and children. She is delighted to have this chance to help kids foster their own appreciation of Shakespeare in a way that is educational, entertaining, and most importantly, fun!

NOTES:

Printed in Poland
by Amazon Fulfillment
Poland Sp. z o.o., Wrocław